Foreword

When you go into a fabric store these days, you'll find bolts and bolts of fleece—every print, solid and texture imaginable. Why is fleece so popular?

Here's the simple answer—

FLEECE IS SO EASY TO WORK WITH

1. You can leave the edges raw (or unsewn).
2. It's completely washable.
3. No sewing is necessary to make a perfectly respectable project.

These are just three reasons why it's fun to work with fleece. You'll discover others, we're sure.

There's a project for just about everybody in *Beginner's Guide to Fleece*. Most of the projects are no-sew (look for the no-sew icon), some require very little sewing and there are a few that are machine sewn. Follow the simple instructions on the following pages, and we guarantee that you'll end up with a satisfying experience and a project you'll be proud of.

Table of contents

Fleece Facts

Before you start, you should know that:

1 Fleece is usually 60" wide. It's important to cut off the selvage edges before measuring the fleece for your project. (See page 6 for squaring up your fleece.)

2 Note that fleece stretches more in one direction than the other. Stretch it to determine which direction is the most stretchy. This is sometimes important for the project you're working on.

3 When using a sewing machine: Since fleece stretches and waves it's important to use a loose stitch (about 9 stitches long). If you're stitching through more than two layers, increase the stitch length. If you're having trouble with the fleece feeding through your machine, try reducing the pressure on the presser foot. Use a universal or ball point sewing machine needle.

4 To trace patterns, place tracing paper over the pattern and trace. Cut out the pattern along drawn lines. Pin the pattern to the fleece and cut out.

5 To mark your fleece, use a marking pencil. They're available in either light or dark chalk so that they can be used on any color of fleece.

6 Laundering: Since fleece doesn't shrink, it's not necessary to pre-wash.

Launder using regular laundry detergent, luke warm water on a gentle cycle. Don't use liquid fabric softeners .

Dry on low for a short time. Don't use dryer sheets.

Iron using steam and a pressing cloth. Don't touch the iron directly to the fleece.

Tools

You won't need all of these things to make a successful fleece project. To begin with, you'll only need your fingers and a good pair of scissors. But if you want to get fancy and make additional things, try some of these other tools that will make your project easier.

Measuring tape
Yard stick
T-square
Ruler
Fabric markers
Chacopel pencil
Quilting pins
Iron
Pencil

Tracing paper
Pressing cloth
Scissors or rotary cutter
Small, sharp scissors
Cutting mat
Pinking shears
Optional: crochet hook,
 seam ripper or rug hooking tool

Cutting and Tying

Square up your fleece

1. Fold the fleece in half, matching selvage edges. Make sure that the fabric is smoothed out to the fold.

2. Place a T-square on the folded edge. Draw a line along the edge of the T-square. Cut along this line.

3. Use a yardstick to measure from this line to the other end of the fleece. Measure and mark 3 or 4 times and draw a line across. Cut along this line.

Tip: A rotary cutter can be used for cutting, but this is for the more experienced crafters.

A good project to start with is a tied fleece throw or pillow. This is a great project for beginners..

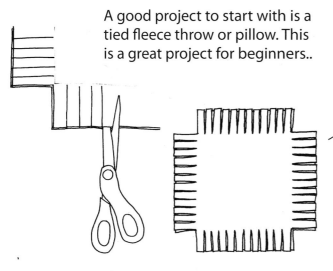

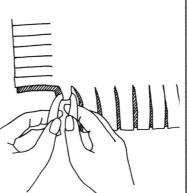

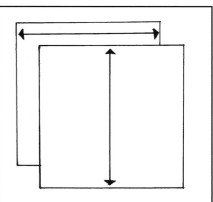

Measure and cut two pieces of fleece big enough for a pillow or throw. Measure and mark 3" for the fringe. Cut the fringe.

This is how the two pieces will look with the fringe cut.

Tie the fringe all the way around for a throw or on three sides for a pillow. Stuff the pillow and then tie the fourth side. (See project pages for more detailed instructions)

Hint: There is a stretchy side and a non-stretchy side to fleece. When you're tying two pieces together, it's best to put them together as shown. This will make it easier to tie the fringe because you'll have one stretchy strip and one non-stretchy strip to tie together.

Fleeces Pieces®

Fleece Pieces® are pre cut fleece strips that can be used to tie any of your fleece projects together.

A

1. Use a seam ripper to make small slits through the layers of fabric about ¼" to ½" from the edge and about 1½" apart. (A).

B

2. Place a crochet hook through the slit. Hook on one strip (B).

C

D

E

3. Pull half of it through until the strip ends are even (C & D).

4. Tie the two ends of the strip together to form a knot (E).

Two knot variations

Square knot

A   B   C

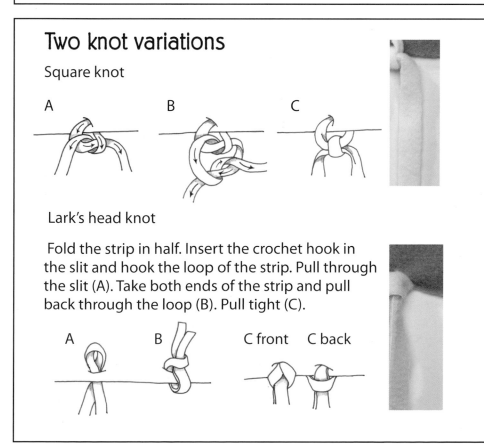

Lark's head knot

Fold the strip in half. Insert the crochet hook in the slit and hook the loop of the strip. Pull through the slit (A). Take both ends of the strip and pull back through the loop (B). Pull tight (C).

A   B   C front   C back

Curling the fringe

Only the fringe cut on the stretchy side will curl. Test the fabric to see which direction is stretchy. Cut the fringe in the same direction as it stretches. Hold the end of each piece of fringe and pull tightly.

Edges

Fringing and tying are great ways to make a fleece project, but don't be afraid to be creative. Try some of these other ways to add decorative edges to your project.

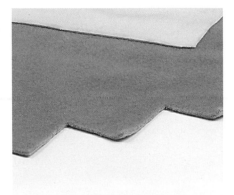

Scalloped: Use the pattern on page 46. Trace the pattern on the edge of the fleece. Cut the scallops all the way around the project.

Hemmed Edge: Turn your fleece under ½" and with your sewing machine, topstitch to form the hem.

Prairie Points: Use the pattern on page 46. Trace the pattern on the edge of the fleece. Cut the points either all the way around the project or on two ends.

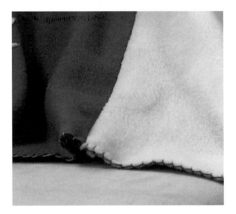

Blanket Stitch

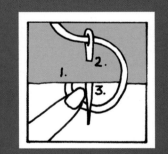

Come up at 1. Go down at 2 and come up at 3, keeping floss below point of needle.

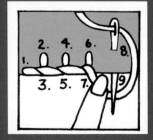

Continue stitching keeping stitches even.

Rotary Cut Scallops: Use a rotary blade with scalloped edge to cut the edge of the fleece. There are other special blades available for cutting edges. Consult your fabric store.

Blanket Stitch: This stitch can be used on the edge of a throw or to attach appliques to a project. Follow the instructions at right to add blanket stitching. Use a sharp needle with a large eye and 4 to 6 strands of embroidery floss.

Embellishments

Make your projects extra-special by adding embellishments. Beads, baubles and appliques can really add pizzazz.

Yo Yos and Pompoms

Making Yo yos: Cut a circle of fleece. Hand sew a running stitch ⅛" from the edge. Pull the thread gently to gather the fabric. Tie the ends of the thread together to secure.

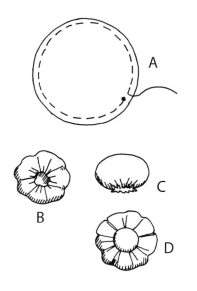

Yo yos can be used in many different ways—right side up with the pleats showing (B) or turned the other way for a more tailored look (C).

Try sewing a small, smooth pompom on top of a larger pleated one to form a flower (D).

Yo yos can be stuffed to form a pompom (C).

Other embellishing ideas:
Rickrack
Beaded trim
Beads tied to fringe
Cords and braids

Applying Appliques

Fusing: To add appliques to projects, use fusible web, such as Steam-A-Seam2. When using any fusing product, always follow the manufacturer's instructions before beginning. (See page 23 for an example of fusing.)

1. To make your own applique design, using Steam-A-Seam2: Trace the pattern on the paper liner. Remove the liner. Check to see which liner removes first by peeling apart at the corner.

2. Stick the self adhesive fusible web to the fleece.

3. Cut the fusible web and fabric together along the traced lines.

4. Peel off the remaining paper liner (leaving the web on the fabric) and adhere the applique to the second piece of fabric. Reposition as desired.

5. Iron for 10–15 seconds using steam and pressing cloth. Move the iron around over the fabric. Check to see if the fabric has bonded. If not, press again.

1. To make applique designs from print fleece fabric (see page 14): Iron the Steam-A-Seam2 to the back of the print fabric using steam and a pressing cloth. Check to see which liner removes first by peeling apart at the corner.

2. Cut out the appliques using a small, sharp scissors.

Follow steps 4 and 5 to finish.

Sewing: You can use a sewing machine to applique the pieces to the fleece. Use a zig zag stitch along the edges of the top fabric.

Applique by hand: Use the blanket stitch (see page 8) to sew around the edge of the top fabric to attach to the bottom fabric. (See page 17 for example of blanket stitch.)

Gluing: There are really good fabric glues available that are washable. If you don't want to fuse or sew the applique, try gluing.

> **Tip:** Both fusing and gluing can also be used as temporary techniques for adding appliques and keeping them in place before sewing.

Pictured on this page are just some of the ways you can add interesting edges to fleece throws. All of these examples are no-sew projects and so easy even a child can make them. The same edges can be used for making pillows. Below is a chart of popular sizes of throws and pillows to help get you started.

Curled Edge: This edge lends a fun and funky look to a throw. You'll be amazed at how easy it is to do. See page 7 for instructions on curling the fringe.

Blankets & Throws

Blankets & Throws	Cut size	Yardage needed
Receiving Blanket	36" x 36"	1¼ yds.
Baby Blanket	36" x 45"	1½ yds.
Child size	46" x 52"	1½ yds.
Teen & Adult	50" x 60"	2 yds.
Teen & Adult	54" x 72"	2 ⅛ yds.
(All sizes include a 3" fringe)		

Note: There are other projects in this book that vary from these sizes. Each instruction will include yardage requirements and a supply list.

Looped and Tied Edge: For a different effect, this looped fringe is a classy alternative. See instructions for this edge on page 13.

Cutting Fringe and Tying:
This is a popular method for making no-sew throws. The fringe is cut on two layers of the fleece and then the strips are tied in double knots. See page 7 for further fringing and tying instructions. This is an example of a round throw. You can also make an oval one.

Pillows

Pillows	Cut size	Yardage needed	Pillow Form
12" pillow	18" x 18"	⅔ yd.	12"
14" pillow	20" x 20"	⅔ yd.	14"
16" pillow	22" x 22"	⅔ yd.	16"
18" pillow	24" x 24"	¾ yd.	18"
14" round pillow	20" round	⅔ yd.	14" round
(All sizes include a 3" fringe)			

Fleeces Pieces: These are pre-cut fleece strips that can be used to tie no-sew projects together. They're fun to use and add a myriad of design possibilities to fleece projects. See page 7 for using Fleeces Pieces. (If Fleeces Pieces aren't available, you can cut your own strips.)

To The Rescue

You'll Need:

1½ yds. each print and solid fleece

 1 Cut both pieces of fleece 40" x 58".

 2 Pin the pieces together. Cut ½" x 3" fringe all the way around.

3 Tie the fringe pieces together (see page 6) all the way around the throw.

In the Pink

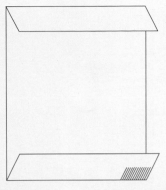

You'll Need:
2 yds. pink plaid fleece
Finished size: 44" x 54"

1 Cut fleece 44" x 70".

2 Turn the edge of each short side up 8" and pin. See diagram at right.

3 Cut ½" x 4" strips along the folded edges.

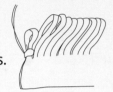

4 Tie the strips in knots to form loops.

Heart Throb (pillow)

You'll Need:

2/3 yd. each purple and
 turquoise fleece
1/8 yd. heart print fabric
Steam-A-Seam2
12" pillow form

1 Cut the two pieces of solid fabric 18" x 18".

2 Iron Steam-A-Seam2 to the back of the heart print fleece. Cut out five. Iron the hearts to the fleece (Follow directions for fusing on page 9.)

3 Place the turquoise fleece with the purple fleece and pin all the way around. Cut ½" x 3" fringe all the way around. Tie the strips in knots on three sides. Insert the pillow form and tie the strips on the fourth side to close.

Heart Throb (throw)

You'll Need:

1½ yds. turquoise fleece
1½ yds. purple fleece
¼ yd. print fleece with hearts
Steam-A-Seam2

1 Cut the turquoise and purple fleece into 50" x 60" pieces.

2 Iron the Steam-A-Seam2 to the back of the print fleece. Cut out about 18 hearts. (Follow directions for fusing on page 9.)

3 Place the turquoise fleece with the purple and pin all the way around. Cut ½" x 3" fringe all the way around and tie the strips in knots.

Target Practice

You'll Need:
Turquoise, pink, yellow and green fleece
Asst. colors of embroidery floss
Embroidery needle
14" pillow form

1 Use the pattern on page 47 to cut two round pieces of turquoise fleece circles.

2 Use the patterns on page 49 to cut the circles for the appliques.

3 Using a blanket stitch (see page 8), sew the round appliques to the round turquoise circle as pictured, referring to photo for color placement.

4 Pin the two turquoise circles together and cut fringe ½" x 3" all the way around.

5 Tie the fringe strips part way around. Insert the pillow form and continue tying the fringe completely around the pillow.

Blue Mood

You'll Need:

⅔ yd. royal blue fleece
Pieces of turquoise, green and
  lavender fleece
Assorted colors of embroidery floss
Embroidery needle
14" Pillow form

1 Cut two pieces of royal blue fleece 20" x 20".

2 Use the patterns on page 50 to cut the squares for the appliques. using a blanket stitch, sew the square appliques to one of the blue squares (see photo for placement)

3 Pin the two squares together. Cut fringe ½" x 3".

4 Tie the fringe strips on three sides. Insert the pillow form and continue tying the fringe on the fourth side to close.

Tip: Sizes of pillow forms are not consistent. You may need to remove some of the stuffing to make the form fit the pillow. Open part of a seam and remove some stuffing.

17

Petite Fleurs

You'll Need:

1/4 yd. fleece (per pillow)
6" pieces of fleece for appliques
Polyester fiberfill
Black embroidery floss
Embroidery needle

1 Cut the fleece into two 12" x 12" squares.

2 Use the patterns on page 45 to cut out the pieces for the flowers. Use a needle and black embroidery floss to stitch an "x" in the center of the flower attaching the flower to the pillow.

3 Pin the front and back wrong sides together. Measure in 2" on three sides and using sewing machine, top stitch all around.

4 Lightly stuff the pillow with fiberfill and continue to top stitch on the fourth side (pushing the fiberfill to one side.) Fluff the stuffing back into place once the pillow is sewn.

Fit to Be Tied

You'll Need:

½ yd. each green, pink and lavender fleece

16" neck roll pillow form

1 Cut the pink fleece and the lavender fleece 13" x 21" (A) and the green fleece 12" x 21" (B). Cut two strips of green fleece ½" x 10" to use for the ties.

2 Fold the pink fleece in half matching edges of the short ends. Sew together using a ½" seam allowance starting in 3½" from one end and ending 2½" in from the opposite end (C). Repeat with lavender fleece.

3 Repeat step 2 with green fleece but start sewing 2½" from one end and ending 2½" in from the opposite end (D). Turn all right side out.

4 Cut fringe on the pink and lavender fleece ½" x 3½" on one side and ½" x 2½" on the opposite side.

5 Cut ½" x 2½" fringe on both sides of the green fleece.

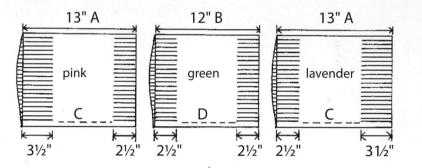

13" A	12" B	13" A
pink	green	lavender
C	D	C
3½" 2½"	2½" 2½"	2½" 3½"

6 With the green fleece in the center and seams lined up, tie the three sections together forming a tube. Use double knots for ties. Insert the pillow form in the tube. Gather the fringe at each end and tie with the ½" x 10" strips of green fleece.

Comfort Zone

You'll need:

½ yd. brown fur fleece
14" pillow form

1 Cut two pieces of fur fleece 15" x 15". Place the fabric right sides together and pin.

2 Machine stitch around three sides using a ½" seam allowance. Trim the seams to ¼". Turn right side out.

3 Insert the pillow form. Turn the edge of the fourth side under ½" and hand stitch closed.

North by Northwest

You'll need:

⅔ yd. each Northwest- themed fleece and black fleece
12" pillow form

1 Cut both pieces of fleece into 18" x 18" squares. Place the pieces together and pin all around.

2 Cut ½" x 3" fringe all the way around and tie the fringe (see page 7) on three sides.

3 Insert pillow form, then finish tying the fringe on the fourth side to close.

Grand Opening

You'll need:

⅔ yd. black fleece
⅔ yd. print fleece
Steam-A-Seam² fusing tape, ½" wide
14" pillow form
4 large buttons

1 Cut one piece of black fleece and one of print fleece 20" x 20". Cut another piece of print fleece 12" x 12".

2 For the window, fold the black square in half. Make a 5" cut where indicated on the diagram (A). Fold the square in fourths and make a second 5" cut (B). When you open it up you'll have an "x" cut in the middle (C).

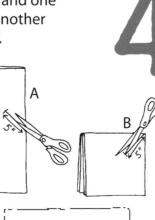

3 Lay the black fleece on a flat surface. Apply fusing tape around the front edge of the 12" x 12" print square. Peel off the backing paper and center the print square, tape-side-down on the black square. Use a pressing cloth and iron the print fleece to the black square.

4 Fold back the flaps in the center of the square and tack in place (D). Sew buttons to each flap as pictured.

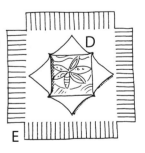

5 Place the black square with window on the 20" print square and pin. Cut ½" x 3" fringe all the way around (E) and tie knots on three sides.

6 Insert the pillow form and continue tying the fringe on the fourth side to close.

21

Fringe Benefit

You'll need:

⅔ yd. polka dot fabric
1 yd. plaid fleece
⅔ yd. Steam-A-Seam2

1 Cut the dot fabric 16" x 20" and the plaid fabric 30" x 34".

2 Iron Steam-A-Seam2 to the back of the dot fabric. Remove the backing paper and place the dot fabric in the center of the plaid fabric. With a pressing cloth over the top, iron on the dot fabric.

3 Cut ½" x 4" fringe all the way around the throw.

My Favorite Things

You'll need:

1¼ yds. yellow fleece
¼–½ yd. baby-themed print fleece
Steam-A-Seam2

1 Iron Steam-A-Seam2 to the back of the print fleece (enough for the desired amount of appliques).

2 Cut a 36" x 36" piece of the yellow fleece using a scalloped edge rotary cutter.

3 Cut out the appliques and iron them to the yellow piece of fleece (see fusing page 9.)

(For a different effect, make a paper pattern using the scallop pattern on pages 46 & 47. Pin the pattern on the fleece and cut out.)

23

Hats for
Kids

In the Clouds

Star Power

Pastel and pretty…these four charmers will keep your little ones comfy and cozy even on the coldest of winter days. Each fleece cap is topped with an original trim—curly bows, fuzzy fringe, or pert pom-poms. They're so easy to make, you'll want to create hats to match their whole winter wardrobe.

Check it Out

Cute as a Button

Star Power

1 Cut fleece 12" x 21". Fold the fleece in half matching edges to form a tube.

2 Using a ½" seam allowance, sew along the top and side of the tube. Trim seams to ¼".

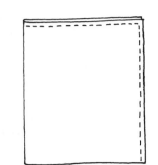

3 Using a pressing cloth and steam iron, press a strip of Steam-A-Seam2 hemming tape to the bottom of the hat. Peel off the backing paper. Turn this edge up and iron.

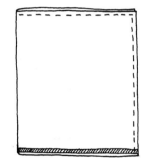

4 Cut two strips of solid colored fleece ½" x 10" long and curl (see page 7). Turn the hat right side out. Tie the curled strips into a bow around the top corners of the hat. Turn the bottom edge of the hat up to form the brim.

Tip: Measure the circumference of the child's head and adjust measurement accordingly·

In the Clouds & Green with Envy

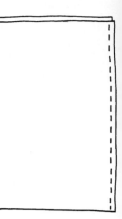

1 Cut fleece 17" x 21". Fold the fleece in half matching edges to form a tube. Sew together using a ½" seam allowance. Trim the seam to ¼".

2 Using a pressing cloth, and steam iron, press Steam-A-Seam2 hemming tape along the bottom edge. Remove the backing from the tape and turn the bottom edge of the tube up 3½" to the wrong side of the hat and press.

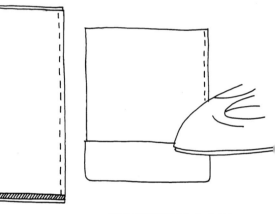

3 Turn the hat right side out. Cut ½" x 4" fringe on the top edge of the hat.

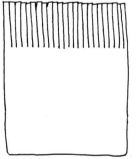

4 Cut a strip of fleece ¼" x 10". Gather the fringe together and use strip to tie around the fringe. Turn the bottom edge of the hat up to form the brim.

Check it Out

1 Cut fleece 14½" x 21". Fold the fleece in half matching edges to form a tube. Sew together using ½" seam allowance. Trim the seam to ¼".

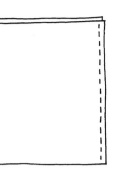

2 With a steam iron and pressing cloth, iron a strip of Steam-A-Seam2 hemming tape along the bottom edge. Peel off the backing paper. Turn the bottom edge of the tube up 3½" to the wrong side of the hat and iron again using the pressing cloth.

3 Turn hat right side out. Cut ¼" x 2½" fringe on the top edge of the hat.

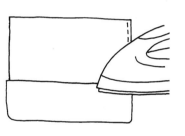

4 Cut a strip of fleece ¼" x 10". Gather the fringe together and use the strip to tie around the fringe. Trim the fringe to about 1" and fluff to form a little pouf. Turn the bottom edge of the hat up to form the brim.

Cute as a Button

1 Cut fleece 12" x 21". Fold the fleece in half matching edges to form a tube. Sew together using ½" seam allowance. Trim the seam to ¼".

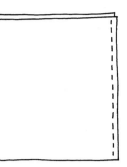

2 With a steam iron and pressing cloth, iron a strip of Steam-A-Seam2 hemming tape along the bottom edge. Peel off the backing paper. Turn the bottom edge of the tube up 3½" to the wrong side of the hat and iron again using the pressing cloth.

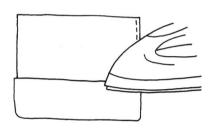

3 Hand sew a gathering stitch around the top edge of the hat. Pull thread to gather and knot. Turn the hat right side out.

4 Turn the bottom edge up to form the brim. See page 9 to make a pompom. Use the circle pattern on page 45. Stuff with fiberfill and sew to the top of the hat.

Hats for Teens & Adults

Hats…hats…hats…perfect for those chilly winter evenings. Made of the softest fabric and trimmed with clever top knots, these hats are guaranteed to keep you fashionably cozy. Softly shaped in colorful fleece, the coordinated brims add some stylish pizzazz. Whether you're heading to the slopes or on a shopping spree, you'll be warmly received.

The bonus is—these hats are so easy to whip up, you can create one in an evening. How about an easy fleece scarf to match? (See a selection of scarves on page 39.)

Warm and Fuzzy

Soft and Cozy

Snug and Cuddly

Adult and Teen Hats (page 28 & 29)

You'll need:

⅓ yd. for crown
¼ yd. for brim

 Cut fleece for crown 11" x 23" and for the brim, 4½" x 23". Pin the brim to the crown with right sides together and sew along one long edge using a ½" seam allowance. Trim the seam to ¼".

 Fold the brim down. Fold the fleece in half. With right sides facing, use a ½" seam allowance to sew the ends of the hat together forming a tube. Trim the seams to ¼".

3 With a steam iron and pressing cloth, iron a strip of Steam-A-Seam2 hemming tape along the bottom edge of the brim. Peel off the backing paper. Turn the bottom edge of the tube up 3½" to the wrong side of the hat and iron again using the pressing cloth.

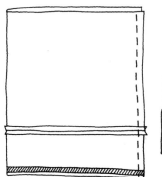

4 Using a double length of thread, hand sew a running stitch around the top edge of the hat. Pull the threads to gather. Knot to secure.

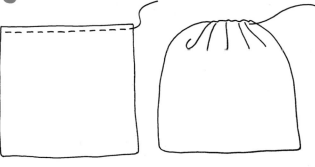

5 Turn hat right side out. Turn up the brim on the hat. See page 9 to make a pompom using the circle pattern on page 45. Stuff with fiberfill and sew to the top of the hat.

Note: The purple hat on page 28 has a pompom made of fuzzy novelty fleece. It's made exactly the same as the other pompoms.

To customize this hat to your size:

Measure the circumference of your head. Add 1". Replace this measurement with the longest one in step #1.

Instructions for this
hat are on page 26,
the poncho, on page 32.

Green with Envy (poncho)

You'll need:

¾ yd. embroidered fleece
4 yds. trim

1 Cut the fleece into a 24" x 24" square.

2 Fold in fourths (A). Place the children's size neck pattern (page 47) on the fold and cut out the hole for the neck (B).

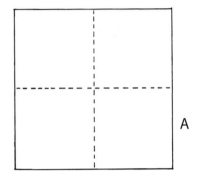

A

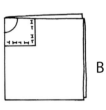

B

3 Sew the trim all around the edge of the finished poncho.

Hint: If you are using a print or specialty fleece that needs to be centered on the poncho, use a large sheet of tracing paper for your pattern. Move the tracing paper around until you've got your pattern centered or where you want the focus to be. Pin the pattern in place and cut out.

Patchwork Poncho

You'll need:

1½ yds. patchwork fleece fabric

1 Cut the fleece 48" x 48".

2 Fold in fourths (A).

3 Place the square pattern (page 47) on the fold and cut out the hole for the neck (B).

To customize to your own measurements:

Use a measuring tape to measure from the base of your neck and down the arm one or two inches below the elbow (or the wrist if a longer poncho is desired). Double this measurement. Cut out a square using a large sheet of paper (butcher paper works well) and pin to your fleece and cut out the square.

Warm and Wild

You'll need:

1 yd. fleece fabric
Pink embroidery floss
Embroidery needle

1 Cut two rectangular pieces of fleece 18" x 35".

2 Place one strip vertically and one horizontally as shown in diagram (A). Stitch together with a blanket stitch (page 8) using four strands of pink embroidery floss (B).

3 Following the diagram, fold the horizontal strip to meet the bottom edge of the vertical strip (C).

4 Fold the horizontal strip to meet the side edge of the folded-down vertical strip (D). Sew together where they meet (E) with a blanket stitch.

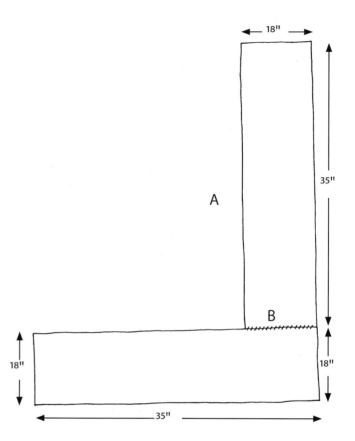

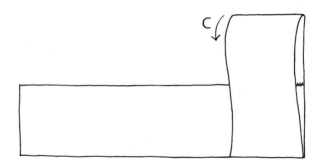

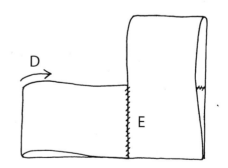

Lovely Lavender

You'll need:

⅓ yd. lavender novelty fleece
10" beaded trim

1 Cut the fleece 9" x 59". Cut the beaded trim into two 4" lengths.

2 Pin the ribbon portion of the trim along the top edge of the fleece and in ½" from the side. Beads will be facing down (see diagram). Sew in place. Repeat at the opposite end.

3 Fold fleece in half lengthwise and sew top and side together using ½" seam allowance. Trim the seam to ¼".

4 Turn the scarf inside out. Turn the edges of the opening under ½" leaving the beads on the outside. Hand sew the opening closed.

Parfait Pink

You'll need:

¼ yd. pink novelty fleece

1 Cut the fleece 6" x 59".

2 Fold the fabric in half lengthwise with right sides together.

3 Sew one short end and the long edge with ½" seam allowance. Trim the seam to ¼". Turn scarf right side out.

4 Turn the unfinished edge under ½" and hand stitch closed.

Basic Black

You'll need:

⅓ yd. black novelty fleece
10" beaded trim

1 Cut the fabric 9" x 59". Cut the beaded trim into two 4" lengths.

2 Pin the ribbon portion of the trim along the top edge of the fleece and in ½" from the side. Beads will be facing down (see diagram). Sew in place. Repeat at the opposite end.

3 Fold the fabric in half lengthwise with right sides together. Sew one short end and the long edge with ½" seam allowance. Trim the seam to ¼".

 Turn the scarf inside out. Turn the edges of the opening under ½" leaving the beads on the outside. Hand sew the opening closed.

Neck Ties

You'll need:

⅛ yd. black fleece
Scraps of yellow, pink, lime, turquoise & lavender fleece (or the colors of your choice)

1 Cut the black fleece 3" x 58". Cut the ties 1" x 10".

2 Make slits every 1½" down the center of the scarf (see photo above).

3 Thread ties through the slits and tie in a knot. Trim ties if desired.

Note: As an alternative, cut the ties short and the scarf will display bright colored dots on the reverse side.

Fashionista

You'll need:

⅛ yd. print fleece
⅛ yd. solid fleece (to coordinate with the print)
Finished size 3" x 58"

1 Cut the print fleece 3" x 58" and the solid fleece into six 1" x 12" strips.

2 On the ends of the scarf, use a seam ripper to make three slits.

3 Thread the ties into the slits and tie in knots. (On this scarf, lark's head knots were tied, but you can use whichever type of knot you'd like - see tying knots page 7.)

More Fleece Ideas

Use the bonus applique patterns on page 51 to create more projects such as the ideas below.

Lap of Luxury

You'll need:

3 yds. fleece with dog-themed print
1 bag each of brown and beige Fleeces Pieces®
Paper for pattern
Egg crate foam pad
Pencil and thread

1 Cut two pieces of the print fleece into 60"
squares. Fold the fabric into fourths.

2 To make a pattern: Cut a square of paper the same size as the folded
fabric (30" x 30"). Take a piece of string (approximately 35") and tie one
end around a pushpin and the other end around a pencil. The distance
between the pin and pencil should equal the radius of the bed (30").
Put the pin at the center A of the paper holding the pencil at right
angles; draw an arc from B to C.

3 Pin the pattern to one square of folded
fabric and cut through all layers. Then do the
same with the other square of fleece.

4 Open each piece of folded fleece. Pin
them together, all the way around.

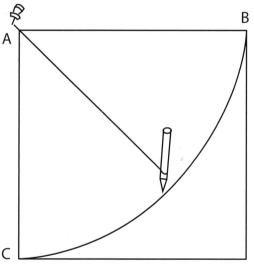

5 Using a seam ripper, cut slits every 1" around the circle 1/2"
from the edge. Leave a large opening for the foam. Thread
the Fleeces Pieces® (alternating colors) through each hole and
knot. (Hint: It's easier if you cut the slits and add strips one at
a time rather than all at once because the slits tend to "grow"
back together.) If not using Fleeces Pieces, cut about 96 - 1/2"
x 6" strips of two coordinating colors of fleece. Use them just
the same way to tie together the bed.

6 Insert the foam and continue to cut slits and tie the
strips until the bed is complete.

Playing Checkers

You'll need:

½ yd. black fleece
1 yd. black/white check ribbon, 1" wide
Black/white check fabric
Black Fleeces Pieces®
Large white and small black buttons

1 Cut two squares of black fleece 13" x 13".

2 Use the pattern on page 44 to cut the scottie dog out of the check fabric. Use Steam-A-Seam2 to iron the applique to one square of the fleece (see fusing, page 9).

3 Place the two black squares together and pin. Cut slits every 1" on three sides, ¼" in from the edge. Thread the Fleeces Pieces® through the slits and tie (see page 7). Trim the black fringe to desired length.

4 Cut the ribbon 32". Pin the ends of the ribbon to the inside top edge of the bag 2" from the side seams and 1" down from the top edge. Sew in place.

5 Sew a white button to the inside of the bag using black thread. Cut a slit on the front piece for the button to go through. Sew the small black button for the dog's eye.

> Note: As an alternative to using Fleeces Pieces®. Cut two black pieces 16" x 19". Cut fringe around three sides of the two squares ½" x 3". Tie the fringe in knots.

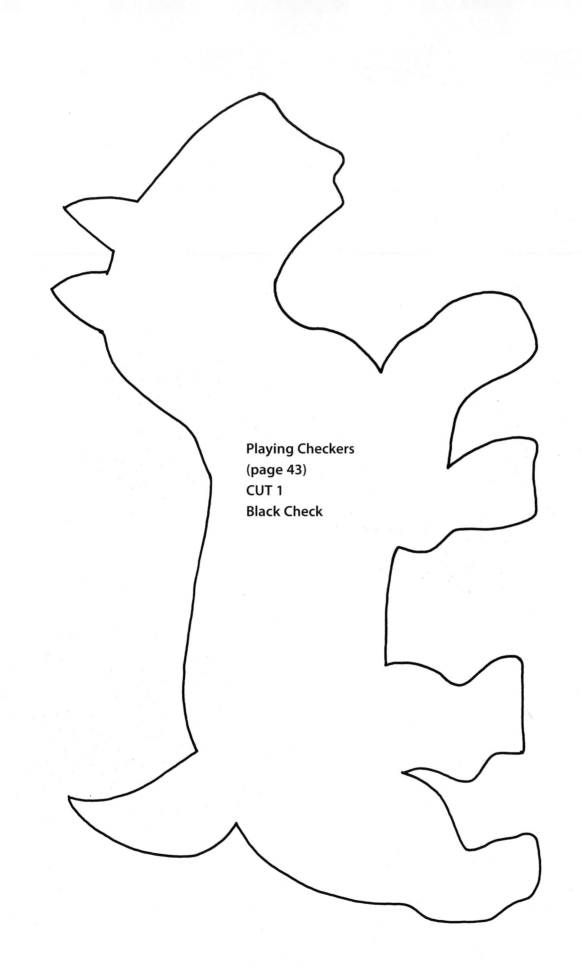

Playing Checkers
(page 43)
CUT 1
Black Check

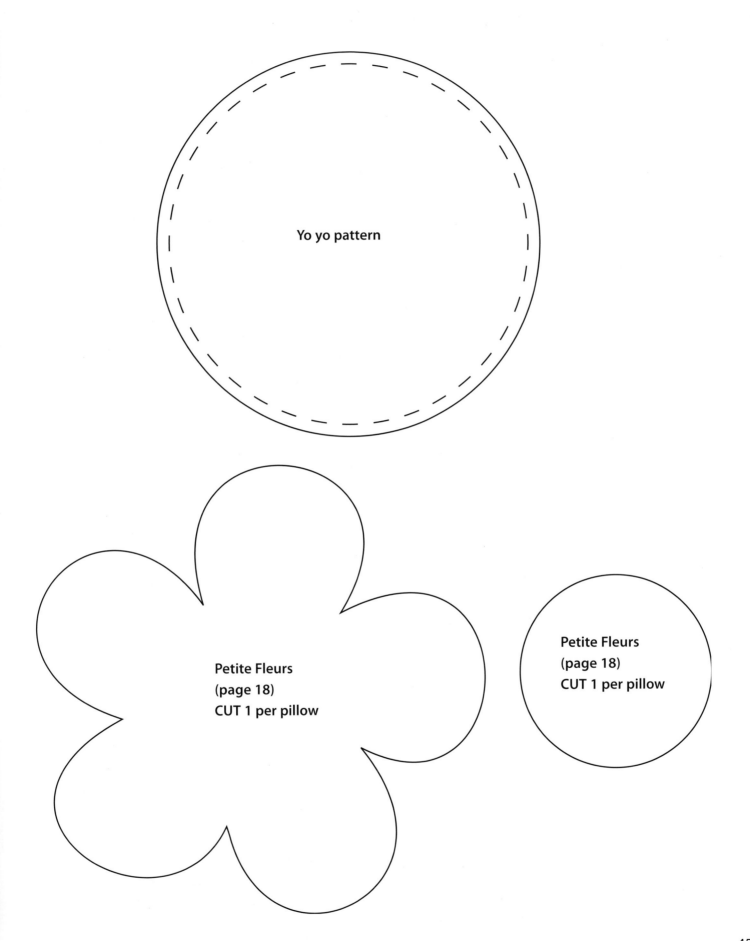

Yo yo pattern

Petite Fleurs
(page 18)
CUT 1 per pillow

Petite Fleurs
(page 18)
CUT 1 per pillow

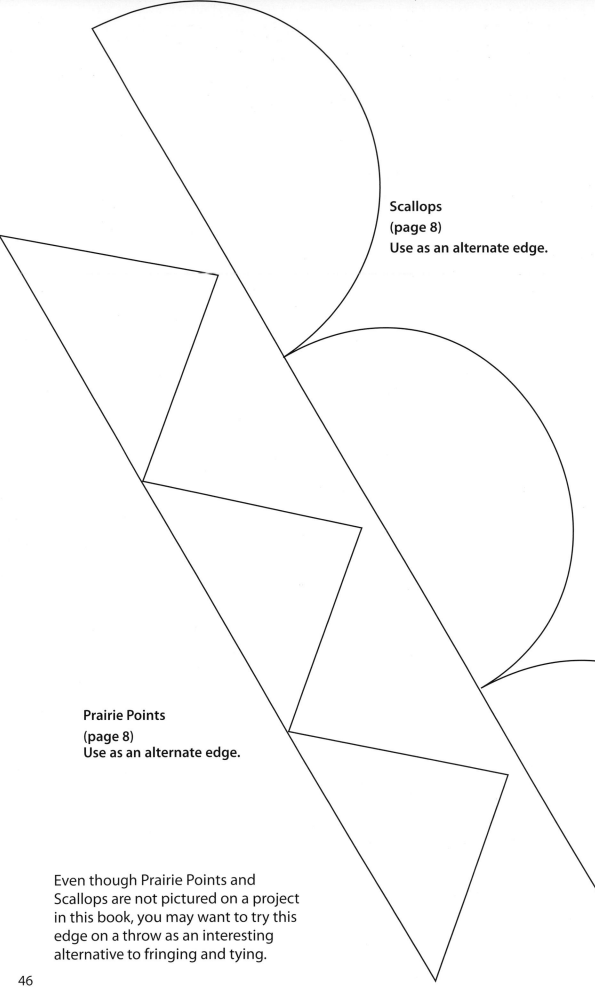

Scallops
(page 8)
Use as an alternate edge.

Prairie Points
(page 8)
Use as an alternate edge.

Even though Prairie Points and
Scallops are not pictured on a project
in this book, you may want to try this
edge on a throw as an interesting
alternative to fringing and tying.

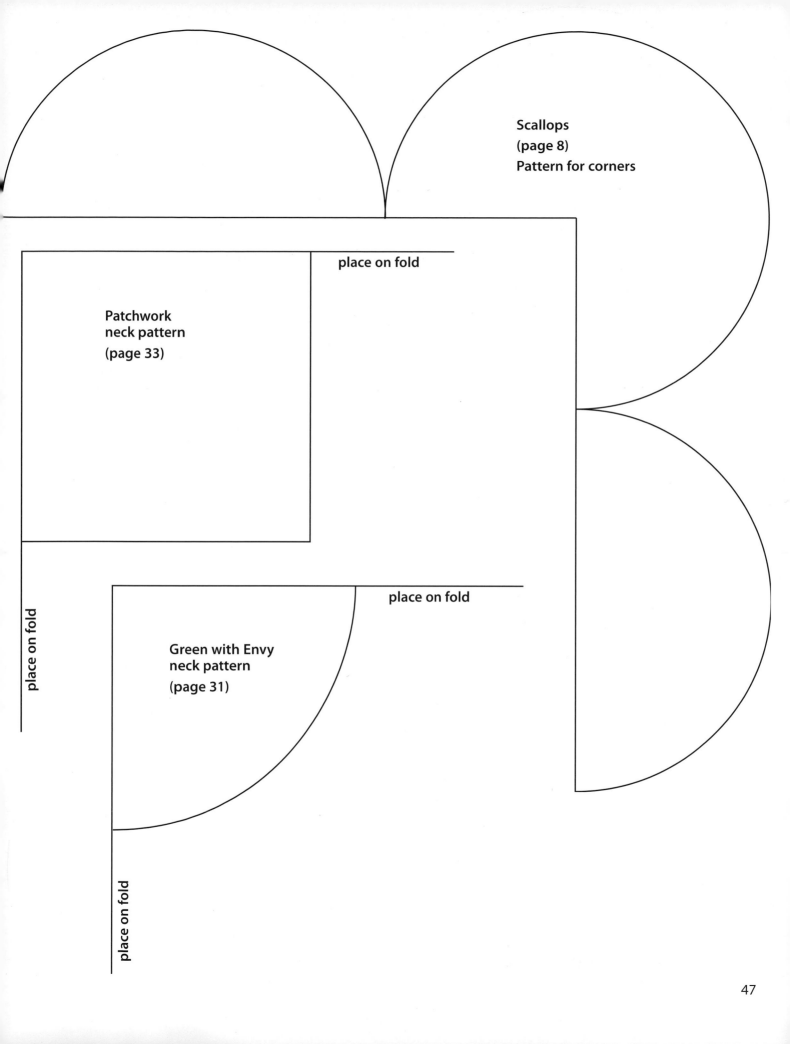

Scallops
(page 8)
Pattern for corners

place on fold

Patchwork
neck pattern
(page 33)

place on fold

place on fold

Green with Envy
neck pattern
(page 31)

place on fold

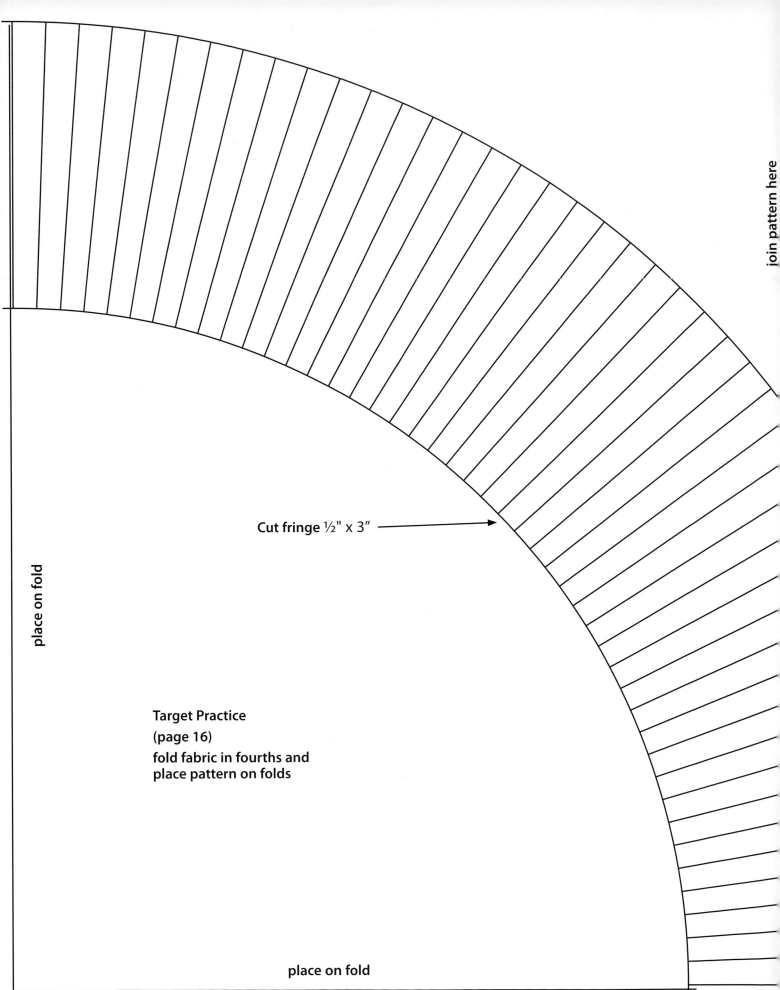

join pattern here

Cut fringe ½" x 3"

place on fold

Target Practice
(page 16)
fold fabric in fourths and place pattern on folds

place on fold

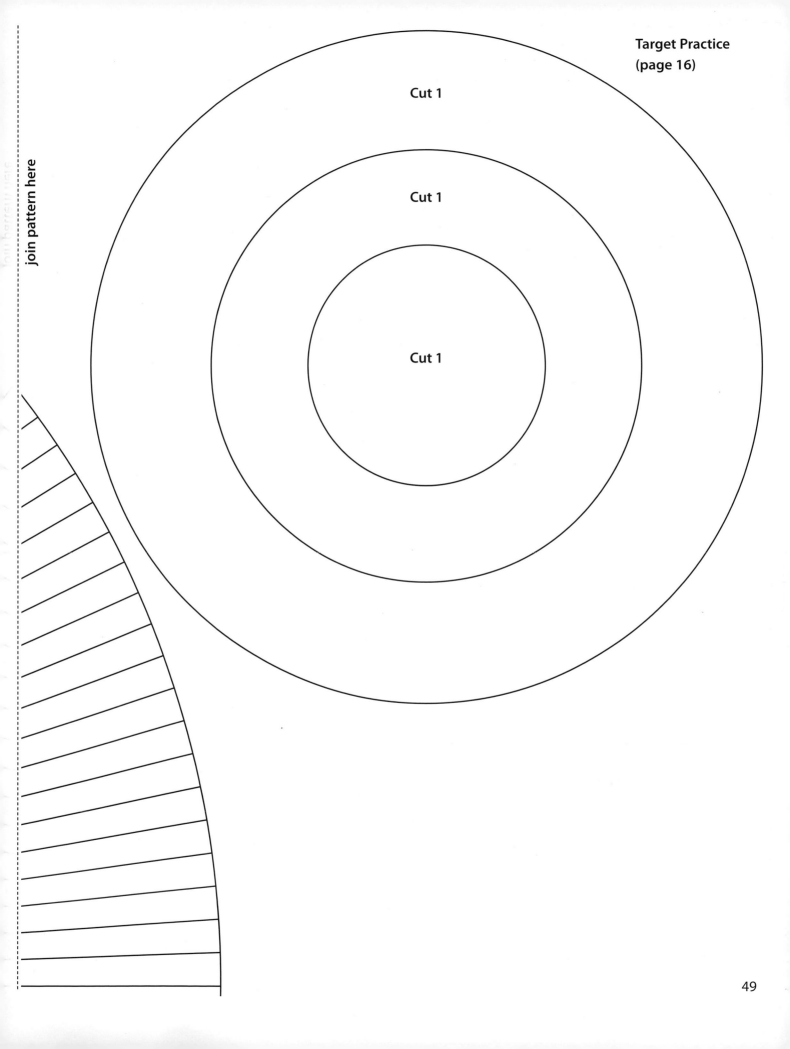

join pattern here

Cut 1

Cut 1

Cut 1

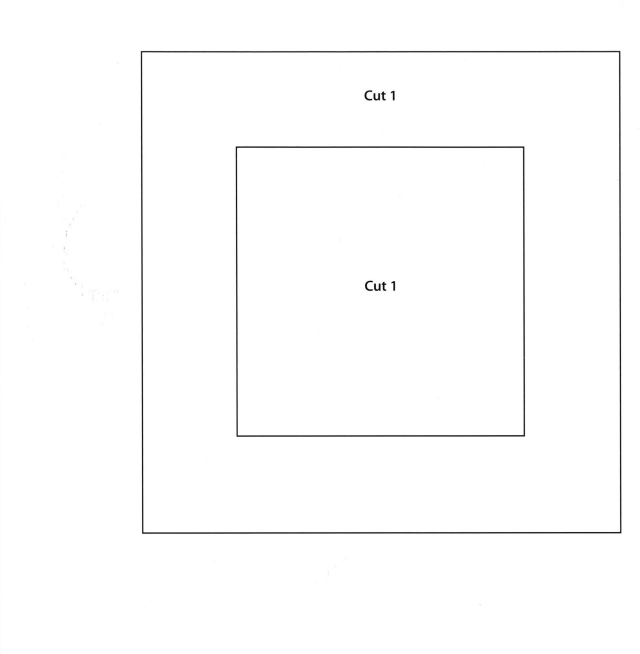

Cut 1

Cut 1

Cut 1

Sources & Credits

Most of the supplies used in this book can be found in your local fabric stores.

If you can't find the item you're looking forward for, consult the following companies to find out where their products are sold:

FUSING TAPES AND FUSIBLE WEB

Steam-A-Seam2®
The Warm Company
954 E. Union Street
Seattle, WA 98122
www.warmcompany.com

TRIMS

Trimtex Company, Inc. &
Carolace Industries
400 Park Avenue
Williamsport, PA 17701
www.trimtex.com

PILLOW FORMS

Fairfield Processing
88 Rose Hill Ave.
Danbury, CT 06810
www.polyfil.com

FLEECES PIECES®

Alexandra Farr/F-4 Inc.
984 McGarry Street
Los Angeles, Ca 90021
800 521 3921
www.fleecebymail.biz

CHACOPEL PENCILS

Clover
1007 E. Dominguez St.
Carson, CA 90746
(310) 516-7846
www.clover-usa.com

FABRIC

My Favorite Things Fabric (page 23)
by Debbie Mumm® for MMFab, Inc.®
550 West Artesia Blvd
Compton, Ca 90220
(310) 763-3800
(310) 763-4777

A special thank you to our models, Aubreanna and Brooke Ochoa and Dana Whalen. Thanks also to Cassie, our canine model.

Banar Designs Principals:
Barbara Finwall and Nancy Javier
Art Direction: Barbara Finwall

Editorial Direction: Nancy Javier
Photography: Stephen Whalen
Computer Graphic Design: Mark Aron

Designs by: Barbara Finwall and
Jerilyn Clements
Project Direction: Jerilyn Clements

Published by

Produced by

BANAR
DESIGNS

LEISURE ARTS
5701 Ranch Drive
Little Rock, AR 72223
© 2006 by Leisure Arts, Inc.
www.leisurearts.com

P.O. Box 483
Fallbrook, CA 92088
banar@adelphia.net